D0437907

More Than
Man's Best Friend

More
Than Man's
Best Friend

The Story of Working Dogs

J 636.70886 OSU
O'Sullivan, Robyn.
More than man's best friend
31994013110926

G

SA 10/06 PL

By Robyn O'Sullivan

NATIONAL GEOGRAPHIC

WASHINGTON D.C.

One of the world's largest nonprofit scientific and educational organizations, the National Geographic Society was founded in 1888 "for the increase and diffusion of geographic knowledge." Fulfilling this mission, the Society educates and inspires millions every day through its magazines, books, television programs, videos, maps and atlases, research grants, the National Geographic Bee, teacher workshops, and innovative classroom materials. The Society is supported through membership dues, charitable gifts, and income from the sale of its educational products. This support is vital to National Geographic's mission to increase global understanding and promote conservation of our planet through exploration, research, and education.

For more information, please call
1-800-NGS-LINE (647-5463) or write to the following address:
National Geographic Society
1145 17th Street N.W.
Washington, D.C. 20036-4688
U.S.A.

For information about special discounts for bulk purchases, please contact
National Geographic Books Special Sales at ngspecsales@ngs.org

Visit the Society's Web site: www.nationalgeographic.com

Copyright © 2006 National Geographic Society

Text revised from *Dogs at Work* in the National Geographic Windows on Literacy program from National Geographic School Publishing, © 2004 National Geographic Society

All rights reserved. Reproduction of the whole or any part of the contents without written permission from the publisher is prohibited.

Published by National Geographic Society. Washington, D.C. 20036

Design by Project Design Company

Printed in the United States

Library of Congress Cataloging-in-Publication Data

O'Sullivan, Robyn.
  More than man's best friend : the story of working dogs / by Robyn O'Sullivan.
    p. cm. -- (National Geographic science chapters)
  Includes bibliographical references and index.
  ISBN-13: 978-0-7922-5940-4 (library binding)
  ISBN-10: 0-7922-5940-8 (library binding)
  1. Working dogs. I. Title. II. Series.
  SF428.2.O88 2006
  636.7'0886--dc22

                        2006016324

Photo Credits
Front Cover: © Rob Atkins/ Getty Images; Spine: © Eye Wire/ Getty Images; Endpaper: © Eye Wire/ Getty Images; 2-3: © Candice Farmer/ Taxi/ Getty Images; 6: © Steve Winter/ National Geographic/ Getty Images; 7: © Alan & Sandy Carey/ Stone/ Getty Images; 8: © Cancan Chu/ Reportage/ Getty Images; 10: © Stewart Cohen/ Workbook Stock/ Getty Images; 12, 13: Guide Dogs Victoria; 14: © Tom Nebbia/ Corbis; 16, 17: © Photo Edit, Inc; 18: © Dale C. Spartas/ Corbis; 20 (top): © Photolibrary.com; 20 (bottom): © Newspix; 20-21, 21 right: © Reuters; 22: © APL/ Corbis; 24: © Photolibrary.com; 25 (both), 26: © APL/ Corbis; 28: © Thomas James Hurst/ Seattle Times; 29: FEMA USA; 30: © Sunset Boulevard/ Corbis Sygma; 32: CaringCanines.org; 33: © Ian Waldie/ Getty Images; 34-35: Julius/ Corbis; 35 (bottom): © Paul A. Souders/ Corbis.

Contents

Introduction
Dogs, Dogs, Dogs   7

Chapter 1
Guide Dogs   11

Chapter 2
Service Dogs   15

Chapter 3
Customs Dogs   19

Chapter 4
Herding Dogs   23

Chapter 5
Search-and-Rescue Dogs   27

Chapter 6
Other Working Dogs   31

Report Guide   36

Glossary   38

Further Reading   39

Index   40

It's a dog's life for this St. Bernard, one of the largest breeds of dog.

Dogs, Dogs, Dogs

Dogs come in all shapes and sizes. Some dogs are huge. Others are tiny. Some have short hair. Others have long hair. Dogs have different temperaments, too. Some dogs are easily excited. Others are calm and patient.

Do you have a dog? They are good company. They like to go for walks. Some dogs like to fetch sticks or balls. Many people have pet dogs at home.

▶ Dogs make great pets.

Not all dogs are pets. Some dogs are working dogs. These dogs are trained to help people. Working dogs learn specific skills that enable them to do tasks for people. Whether it's searching for survivors after a disaster or helping the disabled lead more independent lives, each of these working dogs has an important job to do.

A trainer gives a German shepherd practice in leaping over obstacles.

This golden retriever has been trained to get the paper.

Chapter 1

Guide Dogs

Guide dogs help people who are visually impaired. These people are blind or nearly blind. A guide dog is trained to help its handler move around safely. A guide dog can go anywhere with its handler, even into stores and restaurants.

Many guide dogs are Labrador retrievers. They are good guide dogs because they are calm, quiet, and intelligent. They are trained to look for danger and to follow commands. Guide dogs are trained to ignore other people and animals.

Guide dogs are trained to help people who are visually impaired.

Meet Danny
Labrador

Danny is Joan Smith's guide dog. Joan is visually impaired. When he is working, Danny wears a harness with a handle for Joan to hold. Joan tells Danny what to do and where to go. Joan trusts Danny to keep her safe. If Danny won't do what Joan tells him, she knows Danny can see a problem.

Joan takes Danny with her wherever she goes. She takes Danny in the cab when she travels. Danny even waits quietly while Joan is at work.

◀ Danny sits at Joan's feet when they travel by car.

◀ Danny safely leads Joan when they are walking.

▼ Danny waits by Joan's side while she is at work.

Chapter 2

Service Dogs

Service dogs help people who are unable to do some things for themselves. These dogs help people lead more independent lives. Service dogs are trained to help their handlers in many ways. They can open and close doors. They can turn light switches on and off. Service dogs follow instructions such as "get the phone," or "open the door."

Most service dogs are golden retrievers or Labradors. These kinds of dogs make good service dogs because they are quiet and friendly. They also like to learn new things.

Service dogs help people of all ages with their disabilities.

Meet Molly
Labrador

Molly is Pam Carter's service dog. Pam uses a wheelchair to get around. She takes Molly everywhere. Molly helps Pam do all sorts of things. Molly picks up lots of things for Pam. She can open the front door or help Pam mail a letter.

▲ Molly carries a letter to the mailbox.

Molly helps Pam do the shopping and other jobs around town. Pam even takes Molly with her to help do the laundry. Pam gives Molly special treats for doing such a great job.

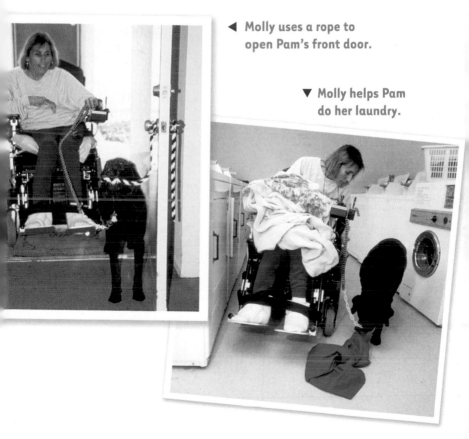

◀ Molly uses a rope to open Pam's front door.

▼ Molly helps Pam do her laundry.

A customs dog checks people's bags at the airport.

Chapter 3

Customs Dogs

Customs dogs work with customs officers at airports and seaports. They also work at border crossings where people cross from one country to another.

Customs officers check the bags of people entering a country. They are looking for things such as fruit, vegetables, and meat that might bring diseases from one country to another. Customs dogs also use their sense of smell to search for explosives.

Spaniels, Labradors, and beagles make good customs dogs. They have a strong sense of smell. They are also calm and quiet.

Meet Gemma
Beagle

Gemma is a customs dog. Gemma works with a group of beagles at the airport. Their job is to sniff bags to find things that people should not be bringing into the country.

▲ Beagles use their sense of smell to find food in people's bags.

◀ Gemma tells her handler which bags need checking.

Gemma and the other beagles know the smell of about 50 different kinds of food. They are trained to sit when they find things that should not be in people's bags. Each dog gets a treat as a reward for finding something that should not be in a person's bag. This makes the work more fun for these super-sniffing dogs.

▼ Beagles work together at the airport to check bags as they come into the country.

Herding dogs make sure a
herd of sheep stays together.

Chapter 4

Herding Dogs

Ranchers live on ranches where they raise livestock such as sheep and cattle. Ranchers use herding dogs to help them look after their livestock. Herding dogs are trained to obey commands. They can herd livestock into a group. Then the dogs move the animals into a new pasture, or field.

Border collies, sheepdogs, and blue heelers can be used as herding dogs. They make good herding dogs because they can see and hear things across long distances. These dogs also have lots of energy and love to run.

Meet Jack
Blue Heeler

Jack works on a ranch with his owner, Bill Harvey. Every day Jack helps Bill look after the sheep and cattle on the ranch. Bill has trained Jack to understand many different commands. When Bill says, "Go by," Jack goes to the left. When Bill says, "Go away," Jack goes to the right.

▼ Jack barks to move cattle around the ranch.

Jack can move livestock in any direction Bill tells him. If one of the cattle starts to run away, Jack will go after it and bring it back to the herd. Jack is a very fast runner and good at his job.

◀ Jack and Bill work together to move the cattle.

▶ Jack and Bill are good friends.

Chapter 5

Search-and-Rescue Dogs

Some dogs work with search-and-rescue teams to find people who are lost or in danger. They may also find people who are trapped in wreckage after earthquakes or other disasters. The dogs are trained to bark when they find someone.

The best kinds of dogs for this job are golden retrievers, Labradors, terriers, bloodhounds, and German shepherds. Search-and-rescue dogs are very clever. They also have a very good sense of smell.

A search-and-rescue dog looks for signs of life in the wreckage of an earthquake.

Meet Ricky
Rat Terrier

Ricky works with his trainer, Janet Linker. Ricky is the smallest search-and-rescue dog in the United States. He is only 17 inches tall! Ricky's size comes in handy. He can squeeze through spaces where other search-and-rescue dogs can't fit.

▲ Even though he is tough, Ricky still likes to be held by his trainer.

Ricky has been trained to search for people in thick forests and in collapsed buildings. Janet thinks Ricky is very brave. He often has to look for people in dangerous places.

▲ Ricky searches a collapsed building to see if anyone is trapped.

Other Working Dogs

Entertainment Dogs

Some dogs work hard to entertain people. These dogs perform tricks at the circus or work as actors in movies, television shows, and commercials. Dog actors don't have lines to memorize, but they do need to follow very specific commands when the camera is rolling.

Any breed of dog can work in show biz. But in order to succeed, the dog must be intelligent, outgoing, and love showing off. Dog actors can't be camera shy.

A Cairn terrier played Toto in *The Wizard of Oz* in 1939.

Therapy Dogs

Sometimes just being around a dog can make a person feel better. Therapy dogs are trained to give affection to people who are in hospitals, nursing homes, and retirement centers. These dogs don't do any special tasks other than lift people's spirits.

Any breed of dog can be a therapy dog. The only requirement is that the dog is friendly and patient. It must like being handled.

Nursing home residents enjoy a visit from a therapy dog.

Fox hounds are exercised before hunting season.

Hunting Dogs

Hunting comes naturally for most dogs, but some dogs are bred and trained to assist hunters in the field. These working dogs help hunters find, track, and retrieve game.

Bloodhounds, pointers, and Labrador retrievers make good hunting dogs. These breeds all have a good sense of smell. They are also intelligent and easily trained.

Sled Dogs

At one time, the only way
to move across the ice and
snow found in polar regions
was on a sled pulled by dogs.
These hard-working dogs
work in teams to pull sleds
loaded with goods and people.

Today most sled dogs work
for sport. The Iditarod is the
most famous sled dog race.
In this event, teams of dogs
race 1,049 miles (1,688 km)
across the Alaskan wilderness.

Alaskan malamutes and Siberian huskies
are the most common sled dogs. These dogs
are well-suited to working outside in the
cold. They also have the strength and
endurance to pull a heavy sled up to 80
miles (129 km) in a day.

▲ Sled dogs take a break after running for miles across the snow.

▲ Racing sled dogs can run up to 20 miles per hour (32 km/h).

How to Write an A+ Report

1. Choose a topic.

- Find something that interests you.
- Make sure it is not too big or too small.

2. Find sources.

- Ask your librarian for help.
- Use many different sources: books, magazine articles, and websites.

3. Gather information.

- Take notes. Write down the big ideas and interesting details.
- Use your own words.

4. Organize information.

- Sort your notes into groups that make sense.

- Make an outline. Put your groups of notes in the order you want to write your report.

5. Write your report.

- Write an introduction that tells what the report is about.

- Use your outline and notes as you write to make sure you say everything you want to say in the order you want to say it.

- Write an ending that tells about your report.

- Write a title.

6. Revise and edit your report.

- Read your report to make sure it makes sense.

- Read it again to check spelling, punctuation, and grammar.

7. Hand in your report!

Glossary

border   the area that divides one country from another

customs   an area at the border crossing where bags are checked

handler   a person who owns or controls a dog or other animal

harness   straps that are fitted to an animal for people to hold onto

livestock   farm animals raised on a ranch or other farm

pasture   a field where animals graze

trained   taught how to do something

visually impaired   blind or nearly blind

Further Reading

• Books •

Dogs and Wild Dogs (First Pocket Guide Series). Washington, DC: National Geographic Society, 2002. Ages 8-10, 80 pages.

Needles, Colleen, Kit Carlson, and Kim Levin. *Working Dogs: Tales from Animal Planet's K-9 to 5 World.* Silver Spring, MD: Discovery Books, 2000. Adult, 96 pages.

Presnall, Judith Janda. *Guide Dogs (Animals With Jobs).* San Diego, CA: KidHaven Press, 2001. Ages 9-12, 48 pages.

Presnall, Judith Janda. *Hearing Dogs (Animals With Jobs).* San Diego, CA: KidHaven Press, 2004. Ages 9-12, 48 pages.

Presnall, Judith Janda. *Police Dogs (Animals With Jobs).* San Diego, CA: KidHaven Press, 2001. Ages 9-12, 48 pages.

Presnall, Judith Janda. *Rescue Dogs (Animals With Jobs).* San Diego, CA: KidHaven Press, 2002. Ages 9-12, 48 pages.

Presnall, Judith Janda. *Sled Dogs (Animals With Jobs).* San Diego, CA: KidHaven Press, 2005. Ages 9-12, 48 pages.

• Websites •

DogInfomat
http://www.doginfomat.com/dog09.htm

Dog Mania
http://www.dogomania.com/category/Working_Dogs/

Dogs With Jobs
http://www.dogswithjobs.com

National Geographic Society
http://magma.nationalgeographic.com/ngexplorer/0301/articles/mainarticle.html

PBS/NOVA
http://www.pbs.org/wgbh/nova/dogs/working.html

Wikipedia Online Encyclopedia
http://en.wikipedia.org/wiki/Working_dog

Index

Alaskan malamute 34

beagle 19–21

bloodhound 27, 33

blue heeler 23–25

border collie 23

customs dog 18–21

entertainment dog 31

German shepherd 8, 27

golden retriever 9, 15, 27, 31, 32

guide dog 11–13

herding dog 22–25

hunting dog 33

Labrador retriever 11–16, 19, 27, 33

pointer 33

search-and-rescue dog 27–29

service dog 15–17

sheepdog 23

Siberian husky 34

sled dog 34–35

spaniel 19

St. Bernard 6

terrier 27–29

therapy dog 32